“Soone [illegible] ant in its
crad[illegible] urse unacted
desires.”

—William Blake, Proverb of Hell LXVIII
(1794)

There Is No Natural Religion (1794)

PROVERBS OF HELL

AND

RELATED SELECTIONS

BY

WILLIAM BLAKE

SELECTED & EDITED BY OLIVER SHEPPARD

ISSUED April, 2021 by Ikonograph Press, PO Box 140551, Dallas, Texas 75214
Design: Oliver Sheppard and Ikonograph Press.

Library of Congress Cataloging-in-Publication data available upon request.

ISBN: 9798736131297

Edition No. 1

IKONOGRAPH IP PRESS

OTHER BOOKS IN THE IKONOGRAPH PRESS
"SOURCES OF THE GOTHIC" SERIES:

1. *On the Pleasure Derived from Objects of Terror* by Anna Letita Aikin (1773)
2. *On Ghosts* by Mary Shelley (1824)
3. *The Fall of the Rebel Angels* by pseudo-Caedmon and Divers Hands

OTHER BOOKS BY OLIVER SHEPPARD

1. *Destruction: Text I* (2017) — out of print
2. *Thirteen Nocturnes* (2018)
3. *Void Noir: Dark and Gothic Erotica* (2021)
4. *Nine Burning Visions* (2021) — upcoming

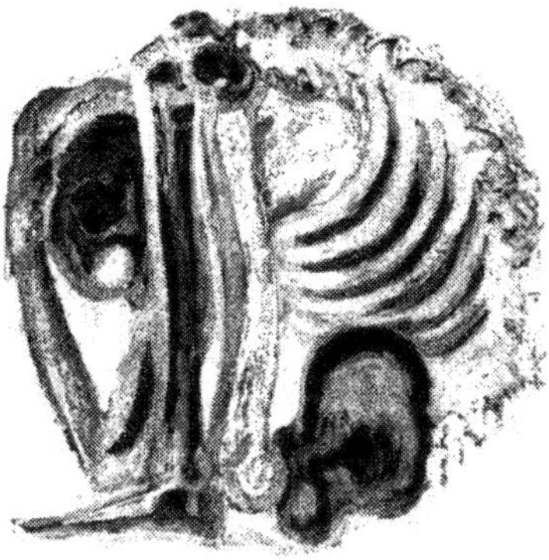

The Skeleton of Urizen (1794)

The Vision of Christ that thou dost see
Is my Vision's Greatest Enemy.

–William Blake, *The Everlasting Gospel (1818)*

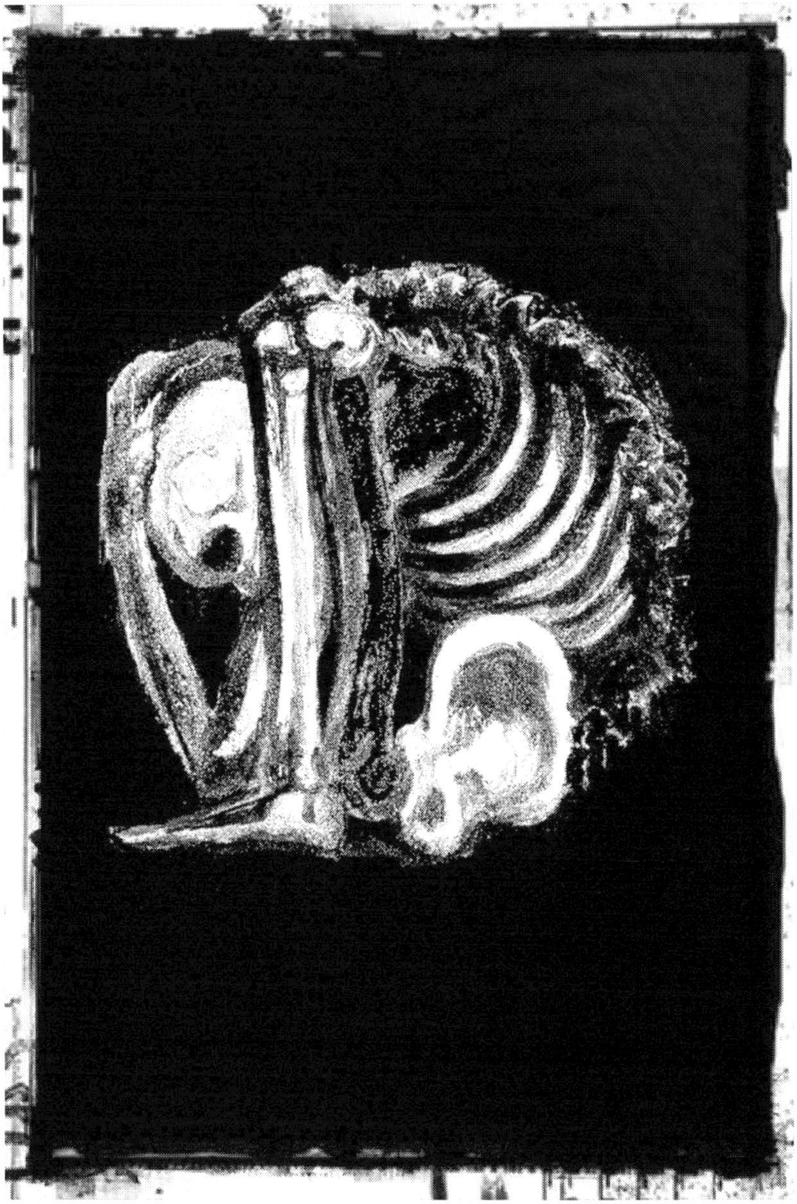

PROVERBS OF HELL

AND

RELATED SELECTIONS

BY

WILLIAM BLAKE

SELECTED & EDITED BY OLIVER SHEPPARD

IKONOGRAPH PRESS - DALLAS. TEXAS

Satan In His Original Glory (1804)

CONTENTS

"I have the *Bible of Hell*, which the world shall have whether they will or no."

—William Blake, *The Marriage of Heaven and Hell (1794)*

ON WILLIAM BLAKE'S *PROVERBS OF HELL*

BY OLIVER SHEPPARD

In 1803, William Blake—painter, poet, engraver, complicated visionary, prophet of grand revelation—was placed on trial for sedition in Chichester, England. Blake, it was reported, had criticized the monarchy before a British soldier; he was subsequently arrested and brought up on charges. Issued by the local magistrate was a bill of offenses that included an indictment against Blake for sedition against the crown. In short, the court's bill elaborated that the humble engraver from London was attempting to upset the established order of His Majesty's kingdom.

Eventually, Blake was acquitted—and when Blake was proclaimed innocent in the court, "in defiance of all decency," the *Sussex Weekly Advertiser* reported at the time, "[the court was] thrown into an uproar by the crowd's noisy exultations." By this time, Blake's reputation had grown to be that of an eccentric, a contrarian—perhaps even that of a wild-eyed madman, a poet claiming a sort of heretical mantle of seer, possessed of visions that revealed the true inner teachings of all spiritual experience. "There is no natural religion," Blake claimed. "All deities reside in the human breast." Helping court controversy were Blake's statements, such as: "As the caterpillar chooses the fairest leaves to lay her eggs on, so the priest lays his curse on the fairest joys."

Nine years before his sedition trial, Blake had published *The Marriage of Heaven and Hell*, a volume that increased his reputation as an unorthodox, and possibly a genuinely subversive, thinker. "I have the *Bible of Hell*," Blake proclaimed in this book, "which the world shall have whether they will or no."

Although *The Marriage of Heaven and Hell* was comprised of several smaller sections, or individual works—works both of prose and of verse, in itself a unique structure for a literary work at that time—specific pieces within *The Marriage of Heaven and Hell* held special fascination (and outrage) for the public. Foremost among these were "The Proverbs of Hell," a kind of antithesis of the Bible's own Book of Proverbs, comprised of sayings that Blake claimed to have learned while "walking among the fires of Hell." Taken by itself, Blake's "The Proverbs of Hell' is one of the painter-poet's most infamous compositions, and probably the single most well-known section from *The Marriage of Heaven and Hell.* The infernal proverbs continue to exert their influence on writers, artists, theologians, occultists, and philosophers to this day. And while Blake's Proverbs are often reprinted as a stand-alone piece in various anthologies of Romanticist poetry, or in other verse anthologies, until now no single edition has been issued of Blake's notorious, infernally-inspired composition.

Most directly, William Blake's *Proverbs of Hell* was inspired by Johann Kaspar Lavater's *The Aphorisms of Man,* published in English in 1788. Blake read this book as soon as it came out and made avid notes in its margins (these notes are available in print now in the "Marginalia" section of David Erdman's excellent *The Complete Poetry and Prose of William Blake*; and elsewhere). "Each particle of matter is an immensity, each leaf a world, each insect an inexplicable compendium," Swiss poet Lavater wrote in his *Aphorisms.* And it is not hard to see how this inspired Blake's own proverb, "If the doors of perception were cleansed everything would appear to man as it is, infinite."[1] Or, even more so, the memorable lines of Blake's later

[1] Of course, this quote is the source of the title of Aldous Huxley's own *Doors of*

Auguries of Innocence (1804), a book that serves as a sort of thematic sequel to "Proverbs of Hell":

> To see a World in a Grain of Sand
> And a Heaven in a Wild Flower
> Hold Infinity in the palm of your hand
> And Eternity in an hour

.....

Of course, Blake was always mainly inspired by the Bible; yet, besides the Bible, Shakespeare, and Milton, Blake's other primary influence throughout his life was the Swedish mystic Emanuel Swedenborg. (One could probably add Dante and Jakob Boehme to this list without much disagreement, too.) Through a series of visions and astral travels, Swedenborg claimed to have gleaned the final answer to all questions of faith, sin, morality, death, God, angels, demons, the afterlife, and other metaphysical concerns. Swedenborg had his grand vision of a New Church heralding the Messiah in 1757, the year William Blake was born—a coincidence that did not escape Blake's attention, nor cease to provide him with endless amusement. Swedenborg's followers established the New Jerusalem Church in London in 1789 on the basis of the Swedish prophet's teachings, and Blake was present at their first conference. Blake would later divorce himself from, and repeatedly criticize, Swedenborg's beliefs—often acidly—as well as Swedenborg's followers' slavish devotion to their master's writ. Blake's repudiation of Swedenborg faulted the Swedish mystic's doctrine's similarity to Calvinism *vis a vis* predestination, as well as other traditional ideas about the dualism of soul and body, traditional ideas

---

Perception (1954), which inspired the name of the band The Doors.

that Blake found profoundly incorrect and even offensive to true spiritual gnosis. (Between Edgar Allan Poe and the Transcendentalists there existed a similar dynamic as that between Blake and the Swedenborgians; both controversial poets mercilessly criticized the two popular metaphysical movements of their time and place, yet both poets' cosmologies nonetheless bear the indelible stamp of these two groups' ideological influence.)

In any event, Swedenborg's multiple "Memorable Relation" accounts of supernatural experiences involving demons and angels—and literal travels through Hell and Heaven—weighed heavily on Blake's own "Memorable Fancy" prose sections in *The Marriage of Heaven and Hell.* In those pieces, Blake likewise detailed his own revelatory interactions with angelic entities and demonic spirits. These "Memorable Fancy" accounts are included in this volume.

The actual "Proverbs of Hell," which precede Blake's "Memorable Fancy" scenarios in *The Marriage of Heaven and Hell*, Blake claimed to have learned from devils while he was "delighted with the enjoyments of Genius, which to Angels look like torment and insanity." (In fact, Swedenborg's *Heaven and Hell* probably provided the inspiration for the quasi-satirical title of Blake's own *The Marriage of Heaven and Hell.*) But even if one of Blake's goals in *The Marriage of Heaven of Hell* was to counter Swedenborg's teachings—or, at least, to provide a more truthful rejoinder to them, as Swedenborg's teachings were much *en vogue* throughout England at the time—Blake's writing in "The Proverbs of Hell" rises above this measure and serves to constitute an awesome literary work on its own merits. Familiarity with Johann Lavater's *Aphorisms of Man* or with Swedenborg's writings is not necessary to appreciate Blake's work in the Proverbs: Blake stands alone, and above—and I would argue also he decisively supersedes—these influences. But for the curious, at the end of this book I have provided selections from Lavater's *Aphorisms of Man* as well as from Swedenborg's teachings. Readers may draw their own conclusions.

Only one (and perhaps even only a very minor) goal of Blake's *Proverbs of Hell* was to serve as a challenge—and, at times, a cheeky and mischievous critique—to Swedenborg, Lavater, and ultimately the Bible's own wisdom tradition as represented in the Old Testament's Book of Proverbs and Psalms. Lest one occasionally find Blake's infernally-inspired Satanic Proverbs too shocking or harsh—for example, Blake's Hellish Proverb II: "Drive your cart and your plow over the bones of the dead"—we need only remember that the Holy Bible itself, in Psalms, contains line like "Happy is the one who takes your babies and smashes them against the rocks!" (Psalm 137:9).

Blake's intent was to prompt critical thinking, challenge received wisdom, and provoke thought about apparent contraries. Blake was compelled to challenge popular thought about spirituality throughout his creative life; at root, he was compelled by an ideal of liberating the human spirit from arbitrary religious limitations. Blake's favorite method of doing this was by way of confrontational, ambiguous, and seemingly-contradictory—and, even, occult—statements. "He whose face gives no light, shall never become a star," Blake wrote in *The Proverbs of Hell.* "Every honest man is a Prophet." And these lines clearly presage the statements of later mystics; for example, Aleister Crowley's famous quote that "Every man and woman is a star." Blake felt that reconciling *apparent* opposites was a key path to understanding metaphysical truths, perhaps anticipating Fichte's notion of the dialectic: "Do what you will—this Life's a Fiction / And is made up of Contradiction," Blake wrote—and this statement is an elegant marriage of occult philosophy ("Do what thou wilt") and Hegelian dialectics. "Without Contraries is no progression," Blake would later add. And it is not hard to see how H.P. Lovecraft, an avid Blake reader, might have somehow been inspired by Blake's line "You cannot go to Eternal death in that which can never Die," and fashioned his own celebrated "crazed couplet" as a result: "That is not dead which can eternal lie / And in strange aeons death may die."

Blake's influence on the Romanticist age of the time (ca 1790 – 1845 or so) is still debated, and although he found a home, of sorts, among his younger Romanticist cousins, Blake was (and still is) *sui generis*, standing firmly on his own outside any single art or literary movement. Byron, Shelley, and the British Romanticists were fascinated with this odd, older printer of illuminated manuscripts, and they fondly considered him a fellow traveler. "There was no doubt that this poor man was mad," William Wordsworth wrote of Blake, "but there is something in the madness of this man which interests me more than the sanity of Lord Byron and Walter Scott."

As with Emily Dickinson's poems, Blake's idiosyncratic punctuation and spelling in his poetry, his capitalization, etc., evince a mind not concerned with mainstream thought. Like Dickinson, too, Blake's work has traits of outsider art. But if we are to say that outsider art has to be made by those not formally educated, neither Blake nor Dickinson can be called outsider artists in a very technical sense. Still, both poets evince an unorthodox fascination with the human psyche relayed through highly individualistic terminology that points to an internal mythos unshared by society at large, and which often clashes with popular belief, or exists stubbornly and personally in spite of it.

Blake's thoughts on will ("energy"), his idea that deities express human inclinations; his idea that the Bible is eminently fallible; his insistence on the mystical nature of Jesus—indeed, his idea that Jesus represents a force we all have within us; and the idea that gods and goddesses in fact reside within us all—these are still challenging concepts for many people and continue to paint Blake as an iconoclast.

Blake was an abolitionist (anti-slavery, as shown by his illustrations), an advocate of free love; and he felt the modern Church's teachings had deviated radically from the intent of the nearly Buddhist-esque type of ethics promoted by Jesus—at least, *Jesus as we know him nowadays.* Satan was not necessarily bad, either. Satan was, and is, a representation of an energy residing in the human person that could very well be a positive impulse in human thought and action. "Men forgot that Deities reside in the human breast," after all. Throughout Blake's writings there is a subtext, as well, critical of the ignorant labeling of things as "demonic" that are not properly understood, a phenomenon that has not abated into our own era.

Blake felt that desire was a positive impulse so long as its realization did not impinge on others' desire and the realization of that desire, either, whether man or woman—or indeed whether any other human at all. Androgyny and hermaphroditic figures feature prominently in many of Blake's antidualistic/nonbinary drawings and poetic sketches. Blake felt that "desire" was a key component of the human spirit—again, comparable to "energy" or the Schopenhaurian concept of "will"— and that restriction of desire was a fundamental evil. "Attraction and Repulsion, Reason and Energy, Love and Hate, are necessary to Human existence," Blake wrote. "From these contraries spring what the Religious call Good and Evil. Good is the passive that obeys Reason. Evil is the active springing from Energy." Tied up in this nearly proto-Nietzschean assessment of moving beyond good and evil was libidinal or sexual energy, which Blake saw as equal in importance to creative or artistic energy. To put it bluntly, Blake felt most orthodox religions worked to quash the human imagination, human creativity, and actively stymied free artistic and sexual expression. I find it hard to disagree with this verdict.

The solution, of course, was to up-end it all; and so Blake announced his *Bible of Hell,* in which he would develop his own mythos, line by line, engraving by engraving, through his own Prophetic Books:

> I must Create a System, or be enslav'd by another Man's;
> I will not Reason and Compare: my business is to Create.

—so speaketh Los, a mythopoeic entity of Blake's own creation, in *Jerusalem*. Unfortunately, Blake's project was left unfinished by the time of his death in 1827.

.....

In 1804, Blake wrote:

> Thou art a Man; God is no more
> Thy own humanity learn to adore

Again, this presages Nietzsche by about 60 years ("God is Dead"), as does its questioning of what is conventionally thought of as good or evil. "Thou art a man; God is no more," Blake says; elevate humanity. Find yourself; explore your energies; realize your powers.

And later:

> Spectre of Albion! Warlike Fiend!
> In clouds of blood and ruin roll'd:
> I here reclaim thee as my own
> My Selfhood! Satan! armed in gold.

We still struggle with, and yet enjoy, Blake's revelations to us. I am abundantly happy to present Blake's *Proverbs of Hell* here.

—*Oliver Sheppard*
April, 2021
Dallas, Texas

Portrait of William Blake by Thomas Phillips (1807)

The Great Red Dragon and the Woman Clothed in the Sun (1803)

The Proverbs of Hell

William Blake

A MEMORABLE FANCY (I)

As I was walking among the fires of Hell, delighted with the enjoyments of Genius, which to Angels look like torment and insanity, I collected some of their Proverbs; thinking that as the sayings used in a nation mark its character, so the Proverbs of Hell show the nature of Infernal wisdom better than any description of buildings or garments.

When I came home, on the abyss of the five senses, where a flat-sided steep frowns over the present world, I saw a mighty Devil, folded in black clouds, hovering on the sides of the rock: with corroding fires he wrote the following sentence now perceived by the minds of men, and read by them on earth:—

How do you know but ev'ry Bird that cuts the airy way,
Is an immense World of Delight, clos'd by your senses five?

The Proverbs of Hell (1794)

William Blake

I.

In seed time learn, in harvest teach, in winter enjoy.

II.

Drive your cart and your plow over the bones of the dead.

III.

The road of excess leads to the palace of wisdom.

IV.

Prudence is a rich ugly old maid courted by Incapacity.

V.

He who desires but acts not, breeds pestilence.

VI.

The cut worm forgives the plow.

VII.

Dip him in the river who loves water.

"A dead body revenges not injuries." —Proverb of Hell XVI

VIII.

A fool sees not the same tree that a wise man sees.

IX.

He whose face gives no light, shall never become a star.

X.

Eternity is in love with the productions of time.

XI.

The busy bee has no time for sorrow.

XII.

The hours of folly are measur'd by the clock, but of wisdom: no clock can measure.

XIII.

All wholesome food is caught without a net or trap.

XIV.

Bring out number, weight, and measure in a year of dearth.

XV.

No bird soars too high, if he soars with his own wings.

XVI.

A dead body revenges not injuries.

XVII.

The most sublime act is to set another before you.

XVIII.

If the fool would persist in his folly he would become wise.

XIX.

Folly is the cloke of knavery. *[sic]*

XX.

Shame is Prides cloke. *[sic]*

XXI.

Prisons are built with stones of Law, Brothels with bricks of Religion.

XXII.

The pride of the peacock is the glory of God.

XXIII.

The lust of the goat is the bounty of God.

XXIV.

The wrath of the lion is the wisdom of God.

XXV.

The nakedness of woman is the work of God.

XXVI.

Excess of sorrow laughs. Excess of joy weeps.

XXVII.

The roaring of lions, the howling of wolves, the raging of the stormy sea, and the destructive sword are portions of eternity too great for the eye of man.

XXVIII.

The fox condemns the trap, not himself.

XXIX.

Joys impregnate. Sorrows bring forth.

XXX.

Let man wear the fell of the lion, woman the fleece of the sheep.

XXXI.

The bird a nest, the spider a web, man friendship.

XXXII.

The selfish smiling fool and the sullen frowning fool shall be both thought wise that they may be a rod.

XXXIII.

What is now proved was once only imagin'd.

XXXIV.

The rat, the mouse, the fox, the rabbit watch the roots; the lion, the tyger, the horse, the elephant, watch the fruits.

XXXV.

The cistern contains; the fountain overflows.

XXXVIII.

One thought fills immensity.

XXXIX.

Always be ready to speak your mind, and a base man will avoid you.

XXXIX.

Everything possible to be believ'd is an image of truth.

XL.

The eagle never lost so much time, as when he submitted to learn of the crow.

XLI.

The fox provides for himself, but God provides for the lion.

XLII.

Think in the morning, Act in the noon, Eat in the evening, Sleep in the night.

XLIII.

He who has sufferd you to impose on him knows you.

XLIV.

As the plow follows words, so God rewards prayers.

XLV.

The tygers of wrath are wiser than the horses of instruction.

XLVI.

Expect poison from the standing water.

XLVII.

You never know what is enough unless you know what is more than enough.

XLVIII.

Listen to the fools reproach! It is a kingly title!

XLIX.

The eyes of fire, the nostrils of air, the mouth of water, the beard of earth.

L.

The weak in courage is strong in cunning.

LI.

The apple tree never asks the beech how he shall grow, nor the lion the horse how he shall take his prey.

LII.

The thankful receiver bears a plentiful harvest.

LIII.

If others had not been foolish, we should be so.

LIV.

The soul of sweet delight can never be defil'd.

LV.

When thou seest an Eagle, thou seest a portion of Genius. Lift up thy head!

LVI.

As the caterpillar chooses the fairest leaves to lay her eggs on, so the priest lays his curse on the fairest joys.

LVII.

To create a little flower is the labour of the ages.

LVIII.

Damn braces; bless relaxes.

LIX.

The best wine is the oldest, the best water the newest.

LX.

Prayers plow not! Praises reap not!

LXI.

Joys laugh not! Sorrows weep not!

LXII.

The head Sublime, the heart Pathos, the genitals Beauty, the hands and feet Proportion.

LXIII.

As the air to a bird or the sea to a fish, so is contempt to the contemptible.

LXIV.

The crow wish'd everything was black; the owl, that everything was white.

LXV.

Exuberance is Beauty.

LXVI.

If the lion was advised by the fox, he would be cunning.

LXVII.

Improvement makes strait roads, but the crooked roads without Improvement, are roads of Genius.

LXVIII.

Sooner murder an infant in its cradle than nurse unacted desires.

LXIX.

Where man is not, nature is barren.

LXX.

Truth can never be told so as to be understood, and not be believ'd.

LXXI.

Enough! or Too much.

The ancient poets animated all sensible objects with Gods or Geniuses, calling them by the names and adorning them with properties of woods, rivers, mountains, lakes, cities, nations, and whatever their enlarged and numerous senses could perceive. And particularly they studied the Genius of each city and country, placing it under its mental deity. Till a system was formed, which some took advantage of and enslaved the vulgar by attempting to realize or abstract the mental deities from their objects. Thus began Priesthood. Choosing forms of worship from poetic tales. And at length they pronounced that the Gods had ordered such things.

Thus men forgot that all deities reside in the human breast.

A MEMORABLE FANCY (II)

The Prophets Isaiah and Ezekiel dined with me, and I asked them how they dared so roundly to assert that God spoke to them, and whether they did not think at the time that they would be misunderstood, and so be the cause of imposition.

Isaiah answered: "I saw no God, nor heard any, in a finite organical perception: but my senses discovered the infinite in everything; and as I was then persuaded, and remained confirmed, that the voice of honest indignation is the voice of God, I cared not for consequences, but wrote."

Then I asked: "Does a firm persuasion that a thing is so, make it so?"

He replied: "All poets believe that it does, and in ages of imagination this firm persuasion removed mountains; but many are not capable of a firm persuasion of anything."

Then Ezekiel said: "The philosophy of the East taught the first principles of human perception; some nations held one principle for the origin, and some another. We of Israel taught that the Poetic Genius (as you now call it) was the first principle, and all the others merely derivative, which was the cause of our despising the Priests and Philosophers of other countries, and prophesying that all Gods would at last be proved to originate in ours, and to be the tributaries of the

Poetic Genius. It was this that our great poet King David desired so fervently, and invokes so pathetically, saying by this he conquers enemies and governs kingdoms; and we so loved our God that we cursed in His name all the deities of surrounding nations, and asserted that they had rebelled. From these opinions the vulgar came to think that all nations would at last be subject to the Jews.

"This," said he, "like all firm persuasions, is come to pass, for all nations believe the Jews' code, and worship the Jews' God; and what greater subjection can be?"

I heard this with some wonder, and must confess my own conviction. After dinner I asked Isaiah to favour the world with his lost works; he said none of equal value was lost. Ezekiel said the same of his.

I also asked Isaiah what made him go naked and barefoot three years. He answered: "The same that made our friend Diogenes the Grecian."

I then asked Ezekiel why he ate dung, and lay so long on his right and left side. He answered: "The desire of raising other men into a perception of the infinite. This the North American tribes practise. And is he honest who resists his genius or conscience, only for the sake of present ease or gratification?"

. . . . .

The ancient tradition that the world will be consumed in fire at the end of six thousand years is true, as I have heard from Hell.

For the cherub with his flaming sword is hereby commanded to leave his guard at [the] tree of life, and when he does, the whole creation will be consumed and appear infinite and holy, whereas it now appears finite and corrupt.

This will come to pass by an improvement of sensual enjoyment.

But first the notion that man has a body distinct from his soul is to be expunged; this I shall do by printing in the infernal method by corrosives, which in Hell are salutary and medicinal, melting apparent surfaces away, and displaying the infinite which was hid.

If the doors of perception were cleansed everything would appear to man as it is, infinite.

For man has closed himself up, till he sees all things through narrow chinks of his cavern.

A MEMORABLE FANCY (III)

I was in a printing-house in Hell, and saw the method in which knowledge is transmitted from generation to generation.

In the first chamber was a dragon-man, clearing away the rubbish from a cave's mouth; within, a number of dragons were hollowing the cave.

In the second chamber was a viper folding round the rock and the cave, and others adorning it with gold, silver, and precious stones.

In the third chamber was an eagle with wings and feathers of air; he caused the inside of the cave to be infinite; around were numbers of eagle-like men, who built palaces in the immense cliffs.

In the fourth chamber were lions of flaming fire raging around and melting the metals into living fluids.

In the fifth chamber were unnamed forms, which cast the metals into the expanse.

There they were received by men who occupied the sixth chamber, and took the forms of books, and were arranged in libraries.

. . . . .

The Giants who formed this world into its sensual existence and now seem to live in it in chains are in truth the causes of its life and the sources of all activity, but the chains are the cunning of weak and tame minds, which have power to resist energy, according to the proverb, "The weak in courage is strong in cunning."

Thus one portion of being is the Prolific, the other the Devouring. To the devourer it seems as if the producer was in his chains; but it is not so, he only takes portions of existence, and fancies that the whole.

But the Prolific would cease to be prolific unless the Devourer as a sea received the excess of his delights.

Some will say, "Is not God alone the Prolific?" I answer: "God only acts and is in existing beings or men."

These two classes of men are always upon earth, and they should be enemies: whoever tries to reconcile them seeks to destroy existence.

Religion is an endeavour to reconcile the two.

Note.—Jesus Christ did not wish to unite but to separate them, as in the parable of sheep and goats; and He says: "I came not to send peace, but a sword."

Messiah, or Satan, or Tempter, was formerly thought to be one of the antediluvians who are our Energies.

"By degrees we beheld the infinite abyss, fiery as the smoke of a burning city; beneath us at an immense distance was the sun, black but shining; round it were fiery tracks on which revolved vast spiders, crawling after their prey, which flew, or rather swum, in the infinite deep, in the most terrific shapes of animals sprung from corruption..."

—William Blake, *A Memorable Fancy (V) (1794)*

A MEMORABLE FANCY (IV)

An Angel came to me and said: "O pitiable foolish young man! O horrible, O dreadful state! Consider the hot burning dungeon thou art preparing for thyself to all Eternity, to which thou art going in such career."

I said: "Perhaps you will be willing to show me my eternal lot, and we will contemplate together upon it, and see whether your lot or mine is most desirable."

So he took me through a stable, and through a church, and down into the church vault, at the end of which was a mill; through the mill we went, and came to a cave; down the winding cavern we groped our tedious way, till a void boundless as a nether sky appeared beneath us, and we held by the roots of trees, and hung over this immensity; but I said: "If you please, we will commit ourselves to this void, and see whether Providence is here also; if you will not, I will." But he answered: "Do not presume, O young man; but as we here remain, behold thy lot, which will soon appear when the darkness passes away."

So I remained with him sitting in the twisted root of an oak; he was suspended in a fungus, which hung with the head downward into the deep.

By degrees we beheld the infinite abyss, fiery as the smoke of a burning city; beneath us at an immense distance was the sun, black but shining; round it were fiery tracks on which revolved vast spiders, crawling after their prey, which flew, or rather swum, in the infinite deep, in the most terrific shapes of animals sprung from corruption; and the air was full of them, and seemed composed of them. These are Devils, and are called powers of the air. I now asked my companion which was my eternal lot. He said: "Between the black and white spiders."

But now, from between the black and white spiders, a cloud and fire burst and rolled through the deep, blackening all beneath so that the nether deep grew black as a sea, and rolled with a terrible noise. Beneath us was nothing now to be seen but a black tempest, till looking East between the clouds and the waves, we saw a cataract of blood mixed with fire, and not many stones' throw from us appeared and sunk again the scaly fold of a monstrous serpent. At last to the East, distant about three degrees, appeared a fiery crest above the waves; slowly it reared like a ridge of golden rocks, till we discovered two globes of crimson fire, from which the sea fled away in clouds of smoke; and now we saw it was the head of Leviathan. His forehead was divided into streaks of green and purple, like those on a tiger's forehead; soon we saw his mouth and red gills hang just above the raging foam, tinging the black deeps with beams of blood, advancing toward us with all the fury of a spiritual existence.

My friend the Angel climbed up from his station into the mill. I remained alone, and then this appearance was no more; but I found myself sitting on a pleasant bank beside a river by moonlight, hearing a harper who sung to the harp; and his theme was: "The man who never alters his opinion is like standing water, and breeds reptiles of the mind."

But I arose, and sought for the mill, and there I found my Angel, who, surprised, asked me how I escaped.

I answered: "All that we saw was owing to your metaphysics; for when you ran away, I found myself on a bank by moonlight, hearing a harper. But now we have seen my eternal lot, shall I show you yours?" He laughed at my proposal; but I by force suddenly caught him in my arms, and flew Westerly through the night, till we were elevated above the earth's shadow; then I flung myself with him directly into the body of the sun; here I clothed myself in white, and taking in my hand Swedenborg's volumes, sunk from the glorious clime, and passed all the planets till we came to Saturn. Here I stayed to rest, and then leaped into the void between Saturn and the fixed stars.

"Here," said I, "is your lot; in this space, if space it may be called." Soon we saw the stable and the church, and I took him to the altar and opened the Bible, and lo! it was a deep pit, into which I descended, driving the Angel before me. Soon we saw seven houses of brick. One we entered. In it were a number of monkeys, baboons, and all of that species, chained by the middle, grinning and snatching at one another, but withheld by the shortness of their chains. However, I saw that they sometimes grew numerous, and then the weak were caught by the strong, and with a grinning aspect, first coupled with and then devoured by plucking off first one limb and then another till the body was left a helpless trunk; this, after grinning and kissing it with seeming fondness, they devoured too. And here and there I saw one savourily picking the flesh off his own tail. As the stench terribly annoyed us both, we went into the mill; and I in my hand brought the skeleton of a body, which in the mill was Aristotle's Analytics.

So the Angel said: "Thy phantasy has imposed upon me, and thou oughtest to be ashamed."

I answered: "We impose on one another, and it is but lost time to converse with you whose works are only Analytics.

. . . . .

"I have always found that Angels have the vanity to speak of themselves as the only wise; this they do with a confident insolence sprouting from systematic reasoning.

"Thus Swedenborg boasts that what he writes is new; though it is only the contents or index of already published books.

"A man carried a monkey about for a show, and because he was a little wiser than the monkey, grew vain, and conceived himself as much wiser than seven men. It is so with Swedenborg; he shows the folly of churches, and exposes hypocrites, till he imagines that all are religious, and himself the single one on earth that ever broke a net.

"Now hear a plain fact: Swedenborg has not written one new truth. Now hear another: he has written all the old falsehoods.

"And now hear the reason: he conversed with Angels who are all religious, and conversed not with Devils who all hate religion, for he was incapable through his conceited notions.

"Thus Swedenborg's writings are a recapitulation of all superficial opinions, and an analysis of the more sublime, but no further.

"Have now another plain fact: any man of mechanical talents may from the writings of Paracelsus or Jacob Behmen produce ten thousand volumes of equal value with Swedenborg's, and from those of Dante or Shakespeare an infinite number.

"But when he has done this, let him not say that he knows better than his master, for he only holds a candle in sunshine."

A MEMORABLE FANCY (V)

Once I saw a Devil in a flame of fire, who arose before an Angel that sat on a cloud, and the Devil uttered these words: "The worship of God is, honouring His gifts in other men each according to his genius, and loving the greatest men best. Those who envy or calumniate great men hate God, for there is no other God."

The Angel hearing this became almost blue, but mastering himself he grew yellow, and at last white-pink and smiling, and then replied: "Thou idolater, is not God One? and is not He visible in Jesus Christ? and has not Jesus Christ given His sanction to the law of ten commandments? and are not all other men fools, sinners, and nothings?"

The Devil answered: "Bray a fool in a mortar with wheat, yet shall not his folly be beaten out of him. If Jesus Christ is the greatest man, you ought to love Him in the greatest degree. Now hear how He has given His sanction to the law of ten commandments. Did He not mock at the Sabbath, and so mock the Sabbath's God? murder those who were murdered because of Him? turn away the law from the woman taken in adultery, steal the labour of others to support Him? bear false witness when He omitted making a defence before Pilate? covet when He prayed for His disciples, and when He bid them shake off the dust of their feet against such as refused to lodge them? I tell you, no virtue can exist without breaking these ten commandments. Jesus was all virtue, and acted from impulse, not from rules."

When he had so spoken, I beheld the Angel, who stretched out his arms embracing the flame of fire, and he was consumed, and arose as Elijah.

Note.—This Angel, who is now become a Devil, is my particular friend; we often read the Bible together in its infernal or diabolical sense, which the world shall have if they behave well.

I have also the Bible of Hell, which the world shall have whether they will or no.

One law for the lion and ox is Oppression.

“The soul of sweet delight can never be defil’d.”

—William Blake, Proverb of Hell LIV (1794)

The Great Red Dragon and the Woman Clothed in the Sun II (ca. 1807)

ADDITIONAL PROVERBS

&

SATANIC WISDOM

WILLIAM BLAKE

Unless otherwise noted, the following proverbs and aphorisms are from William Blake's *Auguries of Innocence* (1804) and *Everlasting Gospel* (1818). Other sources are indicated in footnotes.

I.

The Vision of Christ that thou dost see
Is my Vision's Greatest Enemy.

II.

Your Jesus loves the same world that mine hates
Thy Heaven doors are my Hell Gates.

III.

Do what you will—this Life's a Fiction
And is made up of Contradiction.

IV.

Thou art a Man; God is no more
Thy own humanity learn to adore

V.

I am sure this Jesus will not do
Either for Englishman or Jew

VI.

One law for the lion and ox is Oppression.[2]

VII.

Are not Religion and Politics the same thing?[3]

VIII.

Men forgot that Deities reside in the human breast[4]

IX.

If the doors of perception were cleansed everything
would appear to man as it is, infinite.[5]

---

[2] From *The Marriage of Heaven and Hell*, 1794
[3] From *Jerusalem*, 1808
[4] From *The Marriage of Heaven and Hell*, 1794
[5] Ibid.

X.

What is a wife and what is a harlot?
What is a church and what is a theatre?
Are they two and not one?[6]

XI.

A robin redbreast in a cage
Puts all heaven in a rage.
A dove-house fill'd with doves and pigeons
Shudders hell thro' all its regions.

XII.

A dog starv'd at his master's gate
Predicts the ruin of the state.

XIII.

A horse misused upon the road
Calls to heaven for human blood.

[6] From *Jerusalem*, 1808

XIV.

Each outcry of the hunted hare
A fibre from the brain does tear.

XV.

A skylark wounded in the wing,
A cherubim does cease to sing.

XVI.

The game-cock clipt and arm'd for fight
Does the rising sun affright.

XVII.

Every wolf's and lion's howl
Raises from hell a human soul.

XVIII.

The wild deer, wand'ring here and there,
Keeps the human soul from care.

XIX.

The lamb misus'd breeds public strife,
And yet forgives the butcher's knife.

XX.

The bat that flits at close of eve
Has left the brain that won't believe.
The owl that calls upon the night
Speaks the unbeliever's fright.

XXI.

He who shall hurt the little wren
Shall never be belov'd by men.

XXII.

He who the ox to wrath has mov'd
Shall never be by woman lov'd.

XXIII.

The wanton boy that kills the fly
Shall feel the spider's enmity.

XXIV.

He who torments the chafer's sprite
Weaves a bower in endless night.

XXV.

The caterpillar on the leaf
Repeats to thee thy mother's grief.

XXVI.

Kill not the moth nor butterfly,
For the last judgement draweth nigh.

XXVII.

He who shall train the horse to war
Shall never pass the polar bar.

XXVIII.

The beggar's dog and widow's cat,
Feed them and thou wilt grow fat.

XXIX.

The gnat that sings his summer's song
Poison gets from slander's tongue.

XXX.

The poison of the snake and newt
Is the sweat of envy's foot.

XXXI.

The poison of the honey bee
Is the artist's jealousy.

XXXII.

The prince's robes and beggar's rags
Are toadstools on the miser's bags.

XXXIII.

A truth that's told with bad intent
Beats all the lies you can invent.
It is right it should be so;
Man was made for joy and woe;
And when this we rightly know,
Thro' the world we safely go.

XXXIV.

Joy and woe are woven fine,
A clothing for the soul divine.
Under every grief and pine
Runs a joy with silken twine.

XXXV.

The babe is more than swaddling bands;
Throughout all these human lands;
Tools were made and born were hands,
Every farmer understands.

XXXVI.

Every tear from every eye
Becomes a babe in eternity;
This is caught by females bright,
And return'd to its own delight.

XXXVII.

The bleat, the bark, bellow, and roar,
Are waves that beat on heaven's shore.

XXXVIII.

The babe that weeps the rod beneath
Writes revenge in realms of death.

XXXIX.

The beggar's rags, fluttering in air,
Does to rags the heavens tear.

XL.

The soldier, arm'd with sword and gun,
Palsied strikes the summer's sun.

XLI.

The poor man's farthing is worth more
Than all the gold on Afric's shore.

XLII.

One mite wrung from the lab'rer's hands
Shall buy and sell the miser's lands;
Or, if protected from on high,
Does that whole nation sell and buy.

XLIII.

He who mocks the infant's faith
Shall be mock'd in age and death.

XLIV.

He who shall teach the child to doubt
The rotting grave shall ne'er get out.

XLV.

He who respects the infant's faith
Triumphs over hell and death.

LVI.

The child's toys and the old man's reasons
Are the fruits of the two seasons.

XLVII.

The questioner, who sits so sly,
Shall never know how to reply.

XLVIII.

He who replies to words of doubt
Doth put the light of knowledge out.

XLIX.

The strongest poison ever known
Came from Caesar's laurel crown.

L.

Nought can deform the human race
Like to the armour's iron brace.

LI.

When gold and gems adorn the plow,
To peaceful arts shall envy bow.

LII.

A riddle, or the cricket's cry,
Is to doubt a fit reply.

LIII.

The emmet's inch and eagle's mile
Make lame philosophy to smile.

LIV.

He who doubts from what he sees
Will ne'er believe, do what you please.

LV.

If the sun and moon should doubt,
They'd immediately go out.

LVI.

To be in a passion you good may do,
But no good if a passion is in you.

LVII.

The whore and gambler, by the state
Licensed, build that nation's fate.

LVIII.

The harlot's cry from street to street
Shall weave old England's winding-sheet.

LIX.

The winner's shout, the loser's curse,
Dance before dead England's hearse.

LX.

Every night and every morn
Some to misery are born,

Every morn and every night
Some are born to sweet delight.
Some are born to sweet delight,
Some are born to endless night.

LXI.

We are led to believe a lie
When we see not thro' the eye,
Which was born in a night to perish in a night,
When the soul slept in beams of light.

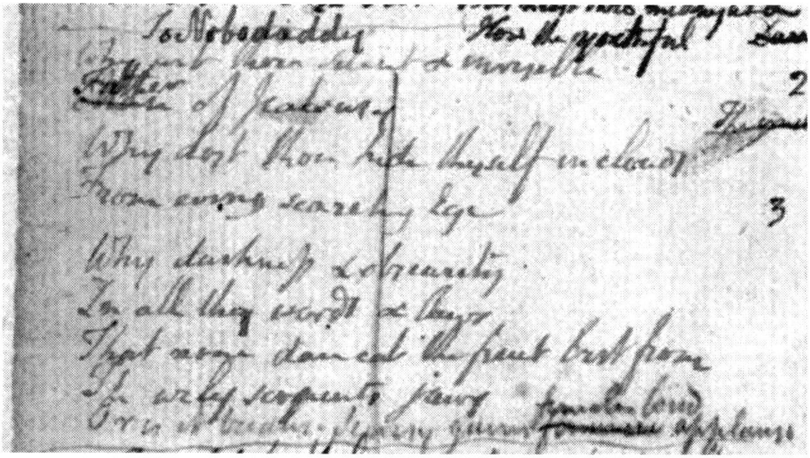

From the original William Blake manuscript of "To Nobodaddy"

LXII.

Energy is the only life. Energy is Eternal Delight.[7]

LXIII.

Without Contraries is no progression.[8]

LXIV.

The iron hand crush'd the Tyrant's head
And became a Tyrant in his stead.[9]

LXV.

He would do good to another man must do it in Minute Particulars:
The General Good is the plea of the scoundrel, hypocrite and flatterer.[10]

LXVI.

Jesus is the only God. But so am I and so are you.[11]

---

[7] From *The Marriage of Heaven and Hell*, 1794

[8] Ibid.

9 From Blake's "The Grey Monk," in *The Pickering Manuscript*, ca. 1807

10 From Blake's *Jerusalem*, ca. 1808.

[11] Statement attributed to Blake by Henry Crabb Robinson in E.J. Morley's *Blake, Coleridge, Wordsworth, Lamb, etc.*, from 1922.

LXVII.

The Modern Church Crucifies Christ with the Head Downwards.[12]

LXVIII.

Severity of judgment is a great virtue.[13]

LXIX.

Man has no Body distinct from his Soul.[14]

LXX.

The reason Milton wrote in fetters when he wrote of Angels & God, and at liberty when he wrote of Devils & Hell, is because he was a true Poet and of the Devil's party without knowing it.[15]

LXXI.

Adam and Satan are brothers. Their father is Yah. יה [16]

---

[12] From Blake's *Vision of the Last Judgment,* from 1810.

[13] From Blake's *Annotations to Lavater's Aphorisms*, ca. 1788.

[14] From *The Marriage of Heaven and Hell,* 1794

[15] Ibid.

[16] From Blake's comments on *Laocoön,* ca. 1826. "Yah" is also variously translated as "Yahweh" and "Jehovah."

LXXII.

Spectre of Albion! Warlike Fiend!
In clouds of blood and ruin roll'd:
I here reclaim thee as my own
My Selfhood! Satan! armed in gold.[17]

LXXIII.

Is this thy soft Family-Love
Thy cruel Patriarchal pride
Planting thy Family alone
Destroying all the World beside.[18]

LXXIV.

A man's worst enemies are those
Of his own house & family;
And he who makes his law a curse,
By his own law shall surely die.[19]

LXXV.

Every honest man is a Prophet.[20]

---

[17] From Blake's"From Islington to Marleybone..." in *Jersualem*, ca. 1808.

[18] Ibid.

[19] Ibid.

[20] From Blake's *Annotations to Richard Watson*, 1798.

LXXVI.

Those who restrain desire do so because their desire is weak enough to be restrained.[21]

LXXVII.

Innocence dwells with wisdom, never with ignorance.[22]

LXXVIII.

He can never be a Friend to the Human Race who is the Preacher of Natural Morality or Natural Religion.[23]

LXXIX.

The Whole creation will be consumed, and appear infinite,
And holy . . . by an improvement of sensual enjoyment.[24]

---

[21] From Blake's *The Marriage of Heaven and Hell*, 1794

[22] From Blake's *Vala, or the Four Zoas*, from ca. 1807, penciled in the margins.

[23] From Blake's *Jersualem*, ca. 1808.

[24] From Blake's *The Marriage of Heaven and Hell*, 1794

LXXX.

"I, in my Selfhood, am that Satan! I am that Evil One!"[25]
[dialogue of *Milton*]

LXXXI.

We are not Individuals but states: Combinations of Individuals...
Distinguish therefore States from Individuals in those States.
States Change: but Individual Identities never change nor cease.[26]

LXXXII.

You cannot go to Eternal death in that which can never Die.[27]

LXXXIII.

I must Create a System, or be enslav'd by another Man's.[28]

---

[25] From Blake's *Milton*, ca. 1810.
[26] Ibid.
[27] Ibid.
[28] From Blake's *Jersualem*, ca. 1808.

LACEDEMONIAN INSTRUCTION

&

OTHERS

BY

WILLIAM BLAKE

TO NOBODADDY

Why art thou silent & invisible,
Father of Jealousy?

Why dost thou hide thyself in clouds
From every searching Eye?

Why darkness & obscurity
In all thy works & laws,
That none dare eat the fruit but from
Thy wily serpent's jaws?

Or is it because Secrecy
Gains females' loud applause?

LACEDEMONIAN INSTRUCTION

Come hither my boy tell me what thou seest there
A fool tangled in a religious snare

IN A WIFE I WOULD DESIRE

In a wife I would desire
What in whores is always found
The lineaments of desire

AN ANCIENT PROVERB

Remove away that blackning church
Remove away that marriage hearse
Remove away that -------- of Blood
You'll quite remove the ancient curse.

"I SAW A CHAPEL ALL OF GOLD..."

I saw a chapel all of gold
That none did dare to enter in
And many weeping stood without
Weeping mourning worshipping

I saw a serpent rise between
The white pillars of the door
And he forcd & forcd & forcd
Down the golden hinges tore

And along the pavement sweet
Set with pearls and rubies bright
All his slimy length he drew
Till upon the altar white

Vomiting his poison out
On the bread & on the wine
So I turnd into a sty
And laid me down among the swine

The Number of the Beast is 666 (1810)

William Blake's own engraving of Laocoön and His Sons, surrounded by Blake's annotations and commentary, engraved and written ca. 1826-1827.

Laocoön (1827)

William Blake

NOTE: I have tried, in the formatting of Blake's writing below, to retain at least some of the experimental feel of William Blake's swirling verse and commentary on his engraving of *Laocoön and His Sons*, which is shown in its original form on the facing page.—
Oliver Sheppard

If Morality was Christianity Socrates was the Saviour

יה [Jehovah] & his two Sons Satan & Adam as they were copied from the Cherubim
of Solomons Temple by three Rhodians & applied to Natural Fact, or History of Ilium

Art Degraded Imagination Denied War Governed the Nations

Evil

Good & Evil are
Riches & Poverty a Tree of

Misery
propagating

Generation & Death

The Gods of Priam are the Cherubim of Moses & Solomon: The Hosts
of Heaven

Without Unceasing Practise nothing can be done Practise is Art
If you leave off you are Lost

The Angel of the Divine Presence

מלאך יהוה [Angel of Jehovah]

ΟΦΙουΧος [Serpent-holder][29]

HEBREW ART is
called SIN by the Deist SCIENCE

All that we See is Vision
from Generated Organs gone as soon as come
Permanent in The Imagination; Considerd
as Nothing by the
NATURAL MAN

What can be Created
Can be Destroyed

---

[29] Commonly taken to refer to Ophiuchus, "the serpent bearer," and a constellation in the night sky as well as an astrological constellation sometimes referred to as the mysterious "13th sign of the Zodiac."

Adam is only
The Natural Man

& not the Soul
or Imagination

Good

לילית [Lilith]
Satans Wife The Goddess Nature is War & Misery & Heroism a Miser

Spiritual War
Israel deliverd from Egypt
is Art deliverd from
Nature & Imitation

A Poet a Painter a Musician an Architect : the Man
Or Woman who is not one of these is not a Christian

You must leave Fathers & Mothers & Houses & Lands if they stand in the way of Art
The Eternal Body of Man is The IMAGINATION, that is God himself

The Divine Body } ישוע [Yeshua] JESUS we are his
Members
It manifests itself in his Works of Art (In Eternity All is Vision)

The True Christian Charity not dependent on Money (the lifes blood of Poor Families) that is on Caesar or Empire or Natural Religion

Money, which is The Great Satan or Reason
the Root of Good & Evil
In The Accusation of Sin

Prayer is the Study of Art Praise is the Practise of Art
Fasting &c. all relate to Art The outward Ceremony is Antichrist

Where any view of Money exists Art cannot be carried on, but War only
Read Matthew C X. 9& 10v
by pretences to the Two Impossibilities Chastity & Abstinence Gods of the Heathen

He repented that he had made Adam
(of the Female, the Adamah)
& it grieved him at his heart

Art can never exist without
Naked Beauty displayed

The Gods of Greece & Egypt were Mathematical
Diagrams
See Plato's
Works

Divine Union
Deriding

And Denying Immediate
Communion with God

The Spoilers say
Where are his Works
That he did in the Wilderness

Lo what are these
Whence came they

These are not the Works
Of Egypt nor Babylon
Whose Gods are the Powers
Of this World. Goddess, Nature.

Who first spoil & then destroy
Imaginative Art
For their Glory is
War and Dominion

Empire against Art See Virgils Eneid.
Lib. VI.v

For every
Pleasure
Money
Is Useless

There are States
in which. All
Visionary Men

are accounted
Mad Men
such are

Greece & Rome
Such is
Empire
or Tax
See Luke Ch 2.v 1

Jesus & his Apostles & Disciples were all Artists Their Works were destroyd by the
Seven Angels of the Seven Churches in Asia Antichrist Science
The unproductive Man is not a Christian much less the
Destroyer

The Old & New Testaments are the Great Code of Art
SCIENCE is the Tree of DEATH

ART is the Tree
of LIFE
GOD
is JESUS

The Whole Business of Man Is
The Arts & All Things Common

No Secre
sy in Art

What we call Antique Gems are the Gems of Aarons Breast Plate
Christianity is Art & not Money
Money is its Curse
Is not every Vice possible to Man
described in the Bible openly

All is not Sin that Satan calls so
all the Loves & Graces of Eternity

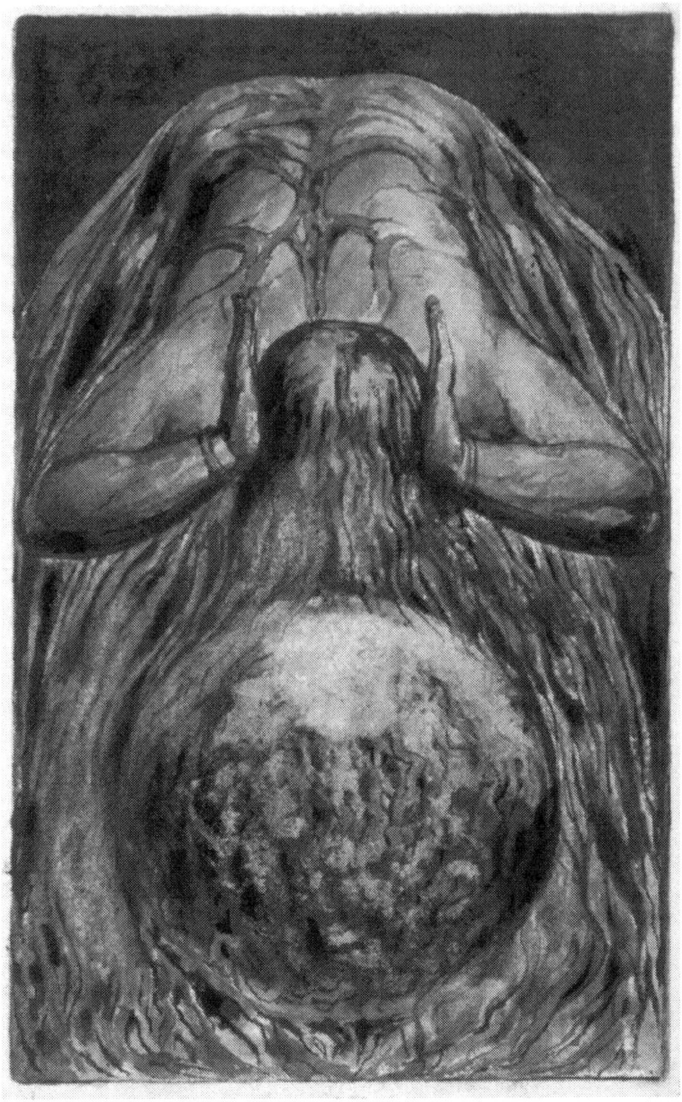

A Globe of Blood, Trembling Upon the Void (1794)

APPENDIX

WORKS OF OTHERS

Aphorisms of Man (1788)

Johann Kaspar Lavater

NOTE: The Swiss poet Johann Lavater's *Aphorisms of Man*, published in 1788 and dedicated in part to his colleague, the painter Henry Fuseli (who was also a colleague of William Blake's), prompted a mixture of immediate admiration and criticism from Blake. It has sometimes been said that Blake's *Proverbs of Hell* was intended as a satire of Lavater's *Aphorisms of Man*, though this does not quite ring true. Lavater's work, however, was certainly one of the primary inspirations for Blake's own *Proverbs*. Regarding his own *Annotations on Lavater*, in 1788 William Blake wrote: "I write from the warmth of my heart & cannot resist the impulse I feel to rectify what I think false in [Lavater's] book I love so much & approve so generally." —*Oliver Sheppard*

Lavater's Aphorisms (excerpts)

Each particle of matter is an immensity, each leaf a world, each insect an inexplicable compendium.

Existence is self-enjoyment, by means of some object distinct from ourselves.

Copiousness and simplicity, variety and unity, constitute real greatness of character.

He scatters enjoyment who can enjoy much.

Who has many wishes has generally but little will. Who has energy of will has few diverging wishes.

Wishes run over in loquacious impotence; will presses on with laconic energy.

Let the degree of egotism be the measure of confidence.

Indiscretion, rashness, falsehood, levity, and malice, produce each other.

Who begins with severity, in judging of another, ends commonly with falsehood. [30]

Who, without pressing temptation, tells a lie, will, without pressing temptation, act ignobly and meanly.

Who, under pressing temptations to lie, adheres to truth, nor to the profane, betrays aught of a sacred trust, is near the summit of wisdom and virtue.[31]

You can depend on no man, on no friend, but him who can depend on himself. He only who acts consequentially toward himself will act so toward others, and vice versa.

Trust him with none of thy self who is, or pretends to be, two things at once.

All affectation is the vain and ridiculous attempt of poverty to appear rich.

---

[30] This is the aphorism of Lavater to which Blake responded, in his *Annotations on Lavater*, with his own counter-proverb: "Severity of judgment is a virtue."

[31] This was perhaps Blake's favorite aphorism in Lavater's collection. In his *Annotations on Lavater* Blake commented "Excellent!" to this line.

The immoderate cannot laugh moderately.

The horse-laugh indicates brutality of character.

A sneer is often the sign of heartless malignity.

I know not which of these two I should wish to avoid more: the scoffer at virtue and religion, who, with heartless villainy, butchers of innocence and truth; or the pietist, who crawls, groans, blubbers, and secretly says to gold, "Thou art my hope!" and to his belly, "Thou art my god!"

Have you ever seen a vulgar mind warm or humble? Or a proud one that could love? Where pride begins, love ceases — as love, so humility — as both, so the real power of man.

Humility with energy is often mistaken for pride.

Who will sacrifice nothing yet enjoy all is a fool.

Thousands are hated, whilst none are ever loved, without a real cause.

He who is free makes free.

Avoid the eye that with rapidity sees the bad, but is slow to see the good.

Those who can value nothing have no right to despise anything.

There is a negative class of people whose constant aim is destruction, who perpetually labour to demolish, to embitter, to detract from something within us; these avoid if you can, but examine what they say: their far-fetched criticisms will often make you attend to what else might have escaped observation.

Be certain that he who has betrayed thee once will betray thee again.

He alone is a man, who can resist the genius of the age, the tone of fashion, with vigorous simplicity and modest courage.

The discovery of truth, by slow progressive meditation, is wisdom. — Intuition of truth, not preceded by perceptible meditation, is genius.

He knows not how to speak who cannot be silent.

The procrastinator is not only indolent and weak, but commonly false too.

The humblest star twinkles most in the darkest night.

Where there is much pretension, much has been borrowed: nature never pretends.

Who has a daring eye tells downright truths and downright lies.

The more unharmonious and inconsistent your objects of desire, the more inconsequent, inconstant, unquiet, the more ignoble, idiotical, and criminal yourself.

The most stormy ebullitions of passion, from blasphemy to murder, are less terrific than one single act of cool villainy.

Before thou callest a man hero or genius, investigate whether his exertion has features of indelibility; for all that is celestial, all genius, is the offspring of immortality.

The greatest of characters, no doubt, would be he, who, free of all trifling accidental helps, could see objects through one grand immutable medium, always at hand, and proof against illusion and time, reflecting every object in its true shape and color through all the fluctuation of things.

Aphorisms (ca. 1758)

Emanuel Swedenborg

There are two loves that have been deeply rooted in the human race for a long time now: love for dominating everyone, and love for possessing everyone's wealth.

Some hells present an appearance like the ruins of houses and cities after conflagrations, in which infernal spirits dwell and hide themselves. In the milder hells there is an appearance of rude huts, in some cases contiguous in the form of a city with lanes and streets.

We greatly desire to rule heaven from our world. All who have a love for power that comes from loving themselves are like this. If we are examined inwardly, it is discovered that we do not believe in any god, but only in ourselves.

Then the ambassador asked him, "Can you make it true that you yourself are insane?" The provider of arguments said, "I could, but I don't want to. Who isn't insane?"

Heaven is not located on high, but where the good of love is, and this resides within a person, wherever he or she might be.

Worship does not consist in prayers and in external devotion, but in a life of kindness.

The more one is absorbed in so-called philosophy, the greater one's delusion and blindness.

Love in its essence is spiritual fire.

We are all spirits inwardly. This is what's alive in the body, not the body on its own.

The essence of love is that what is ours should belong to someone else. Feeling the joy of someone else as joy within ourselves-that is loving.

A person who governs out of love of self does not intend what is good to anyone, only to himself. Any useful services he fulfills are for his own prestige and glory, which are the only things he finds useful.

New Proverbs of Hell (2018)

Oliver Sheppard

CANTO OF ASMODEUS

(—or; New Proverbs of Hell)

NOTE: An earlier version of "Canto of Asmodeus / New Proverbs of Hell" originally appeared in 2018's *Thirteen Nocturnes.*

ARGUMENT

In *The Marriage of Heaven and Hell,* William Blake wrote, "As I was walking among the fires of Hell ... I collected some of their Proverbs; thinking that as the sayings used in a nation mark its character, so the *Proverbs of Hell* show the nature of Infernal wisdom better than any description of buildings or garments." My own encounter with Asmodeus one night—in a quiet grove ringed by dead, leafless, and gnarled live oak trees in East Texas—yielded these further Proverbs from the Infernal Country at the celestial nadir.

In far East Texas there's
A town called Elysian Fields, so-named
By a Captain from New Orleans who,
In the 1830s, found the spot to be a
Perfect idyll. Once, I traveled there *en route*
To Louisiana and stopped by a
Trailer park to rest. Just outside the edge
Of the trailer park two dead Live-Oaks

Formed a sort of massive pair of Horns,
Noticeable from the Highway.
And in the crook of the two horn-like Trees,
There sat Asmodeus, whittling—
Whistling, whittling, and waiting.
'There are Proverbs and Psalms of
Hell for people such as yourself,' he said
While turning to me. 'Which do you
Want?' 'Proverbs,' I answered.
'*Praesignis!* The Psalms will be spoken later.'

I.

Individuality is a blessing. It spares us the knowledge Others' thoughts.

Be not proud of who you are. Is the Pupa proud of itself? No—it wants to become a Butterfly!

Praise the Coffin-Worm for its appetite. Excoriate the Flower for its pride.

Blessed are the Deaf: They cannot hear Others' lies. Blessed are the Mute—they cannot speak them.

Terrible are the actions of Men. But worse are Men's thoughts.

The desire for Vengeance—a healthy regard for the Self.

Propriety denies. Evil allows.

The scheming of Others will be revealed to All in time.

Desire without action is Life unlived; and Life unlived is properly called Death.

II.

Let him who tolls the Bell be first to respond to its ringing.

The Moon is a grateful planet—grateful that nothing lives on it!

Emptiness of Soul is not a curse; the Soul is a Chimæra.

War is the State of Nature. Peace is the State of Exception.

The gardens of Orthodoxy are fragrant with hypocrisy. The groves of Heterodoxy are sumptuous with truth.

Sunlight burns. Moonlight heals.

Take heed: Be wary of those easily roused to Anger by things they do not understand.

The Home represents Danger. The Fortress represents Strength. The Dragon represents Friendship.

Could Humanity but look into its collective heart, War would never cease.

III.

Let him who organizes the race, run it. Let him who prepares the meal, devour it. Let him who finds the lost article, keep it.

Most of that which is human is Ugliness, and is Undesirable.

Poverty is a gift to man; it teaches Innovation. But lucky are those born in the shadow of Death, the most sublime Teacher!

As the tree lets go of its heaviest fruit, so should one let go of their heaviest burdens.

The greater the Mask, the greater the Person.

Destruction: Without it, there is nothing. And with only Destruction, there is also nothing.

The Sun would be just as content without the Earth buzzing about it.

The Self is a fortress assailed by all Else.

There is much that is marvelous that is wicked.

As drowsiness is to Sleep, so Peace is to War.

IV.

The Blind Man seeks Wisdom in Images; the Deaf Man seeks Wisdom in Music. The Wise Man seeks wisdom in No-thing.

To the unenlightened, power comes from strength. But the wise know true strength comes from deception.

They say that youth is wasted on the young. Ah, but death is wasted on the dead!

Happy is he who takes your babies and smashes them against the rocks![32]

We agree with aphorisms and call them "truisms" so much as they reinforce sentiments already held. But we recklessly cast aside wisdom that disagrees with our preconceptions or unexamined biases.

The tree is not resentful of the birds that take its fruits. Be like the tree!

The shadow of Life is Death; and Death evinces its jealousy of Life through the phenomenon of Disease.

Earth circles a Brightness. But that Brightness circles a Darkness, and that Darkness spins along the gyre of a Greater Darkness outside it.

---

[32] From Psalm 137:9 - New Living Translation of the Holy Bible.

William Blake's ledger stone in Islington at Bunhill Fields.

ABOUT THE AUTHOR

William Blake was a prophet, visionary, poet, and artist born in London, England in 1757. Blake produced engravings and manuscripts that combined poetry, prose, and art in the form of illuminated texts. Blake's works and poetry were almost forgotten until Alexander Gilchrist's *Life of William Blake* in the 1860s helped resuscitate Blake's reputation. Since then, Blake has been regarded a major influence on English literature along the lines of John Donne and John Milton. Blake's "Proverbs of Hell" was published in 1794 as a major component of *The Marriage of Heaven and Hell.* "The Proverbs of Hell" are here presented as a stand-alone text.

Printed in Great Britain
by Amazon

62213134R00064